Spiralizer Cookbook

Easy, Delicious, and Healthy Recipes for Your Spiralizer

Savannah Gibbs

The trademarks that are used are without any consent, and the publication of the trademark is without permission or backing by the trademark owner. All trademarks and brands within this book are for clarifying purposes only and are owned by the owners themselves, not affiliated with this document.

ISBN: 978-1-64842-094-8

Table of Contents

Chapter 1: How to Use a Spiralizer

If you love noodles and pasta but you're trying hard to limit the unhealthy carbohydrates you eat, there's a new food trend that might help. It's spiralizing. The concept is simple; you take a healthy food and use a spiralizer to help it mimic other, less healthy foods. For example, you can bring spaghetti back into your life by using squash noodles instead of those made from flour. Learning how to use a spiralizer might seem a little intimidating, but it doesn't have to be. Once you get the hang of it, you'll be cooking and eating in new and tasty ways.

Explaining the Spiralizer

Buy a spiralizer in your favorite department store or retailer selling home goods. You can also find a number of different brands and price ranges online. You shouldn't have to pay more than $40 to $60 for a high-quality cooking tool that can do the job. The machine, which doesn't take up too much counter or cupboard space, turns fresh fruits and vegetables into long spiral pieces, which usually resemble noodles.

It might help you to visualize a pencil sharpener. You put the pencil in, then you turn the crank and pretty ribbons of pencil shavings begin to accumulate. The spiralizer embraces the same idea. It grinds your firm, fresh fruit or vegetable into ribbons without adding anything or compromising the health benefits of the food.

The spiralizer has become a favored tool of home chefs who are trying to cook creatively without a lot of carbs, refined sugars, and gluten. It's also becoming commonplace in the restaurant industry. Mandolin slicers are being replaced with spiralizers because the results are more appealing and there are extra options for what to do with the food once it's shaved and spiraled into these wafer thin slices or long, thick ribbons.

The Benefits of Using a Spiralizer

Knowing how to use a spiralizer can have an impact on your meals, snacks, and general approach to food and healthy eating. If you're wondering why you should bother, there are a few excellent benefits to spiralizing fruits and vegetables.

You can make produce pasta anytime you want. With vegetables such as squash, zucchini, eggplant and sweet potatoes, you can create one of your best comfort foods without the heavy bloat that often comes with polishing off a plate of macaroni.

It's fun! There's nothing wrong with playing with your food as an adult. Twirling your fruits and veggies around your fork can make the meal a lot more enjoyable than just poking them with a fork or scooping them up with a spoon.

The spiralizer allows you to introduce healthy alternatives into your meals. You don't have to have every dinner plate revolve around the meat and potatoes. Instead, you can pile the plate with fresh, healthy, and even organic produce, but you don't have to feel like you're eating a glorified salad all the time. The spiralizer is another tool that you can use to keep yourself with eating better, feeling fitter, and committing to a healthier lifestyle.

If you're trying to lose weight or maintain weight that you've recently lost, spiralizing can be beneficial. The fruits and veggies you spiralize will be low in calories, fat, and carbs, and full of water and fiber. You'll be able to clear your system of any toxins, fat, and metals that you don't want floating around.

Another benefit of spiralizing food is the impact you have on the environment. It's a clean way of eating and it reduces the footprint that's left behind when we consume meat from factory farms and processed foods out of warehouses and laboratories. You can support your local economy by buying the produce you'll use at local farmers markets and coops, where there's a higher ethical standard and almost always a better quality of food. Using seasonal, local foods to spiral will keep you on an environmentally friendly track and keep you feeling good about your participation in the local community.

The Best Vegetables and Fruits to Spiralize

Understanding the best fruits and vegetables for this product is critical in knowing how to use a spiralizer. Fresh fruits and vegetables are best, and the most successful recipes can be made with those foods that are firm, consistent in texture, and not prone to turning to mush or liquid. Some of the best recipes for spiralized food come from these types of fruits and veggies:

Carrot
Cucumber
Celery
Broccoli stem
Cauliflower stem
Rutabaga
Zucchini
Squash
Eggplant
Potato
Sweet Potato
Apples
Pears
Onions
Pumpkin
Radish
Beets

Be careful of foods that are soft or prone to producing a lot of liquid. For example, you're not going to get great results if you try a tomato, banana, pineapple, or watermelon in your spiralizer.

Different Types of Spiralizers

There are different types of spiralizers on the market, and the one you choose will depend on what you want to do with it and how often you want to use it.

A **handheld spiralizer** is a basic and simple place to start. The handheld variety is cheap, takes up very little space, and can easily accommodate small amounts of vegetables. You'll need to make an effort by cranking it yourself, so the handheld type is best for people who only plan to spiralize a little at a time.

Horizontal spiralizers are larger, and they hold the fruit or vegetable in place for you. There's also a function that takes out the core, which is helpful when you want to avoid seeds and fibers.

You can also choose a **vertical spiralizer**, which allows the fruit or vegetable to stay in place right on top of the blade, which makes it easier for you to accomplish what you need to do with any size and shape of food.

Blade Choices

There are also several different blades to choose from. Many spiralizers will come with a few of these attachments, and there are also separate blades that you can purchase on your own. Just make sure they're compatible with the type of spiralizer that you own. Try the slicing blade when you're less interested in ribbons that resemble pasta and all you really want are thinly sliced shreds of food. There's also the thin noodle attachment and the thick noodle attachment, both of which will allow you to customize the type of noodle you're trying to recreate.

Tips for Using a Spiralizer

Use bigger vegetables or fruits

If you want to get perfect spirals, you need to use foods that are slightly larger than average in diameter. You can easily get zucchinis or cucumbers with a large diameter, but you can't always find carrots that thick. Therefore, it is a good idea to buy loose carrots and search for thick ones rather than buying bundled carrots. On the other hand, if you use veggies that are too big, you will have a hard time fitting them in the spiralizer.

Wash your vegetables and fruits before spiralizing

Always remember to wash your veggies and fruits thoroughly before spiralizing them. Cut off unsymmetrical ends so that spiralization is smooth.

Keep your veggies on the center

This is common sense, but it is crucial to place your vegetables right at the center of the spiralizer. It's not easy to always keep them centered, but with a little practice, you will be able to do this. When the veggies are placed on the middle of the blade, it results in continuous noodles rather than broken strands.

Remove excess water after spiralizing

Some vegetables, like zucchini, contain a lot of water weight, which can be drained out. Hence, after spiralizing, sprinkle them with a little salt and let the veggies stand on a strainer for about 15–20 minutes. Soon they will start releasing their excess water, which you can drain off.

Be Creative

Once you get started, be creative. You'll get the most out of your spiralizer when you aren't afraid to try new things. If you're going for a noodle type of dish, remember that sauces are important. Feel free to cover your spiralized veggies or fruits with tomato sauce, diced meats, or even cheese. Check out the recipes in this book and from other sources so you can keep things interesting.

Working with a spiralizer will be fun and fresh. You'll learn how to eat healthy, explore all the different options and menus, and share your creations with family and friends.

Chapter 2: Pasta Recipes for Spiralizers

One of the most popular ways to use a spiralizer is with pasta recipes. Whether you want to replace pasta noodles with vegetable noodles or you'd like to enhance your real noodle dishes with shavings of fruits and vegetables, your spiralizing tool will help you achieve pasta dishes that are healthy and tasty.

Zucchini Pasta with Parmesan

Yield: 4 servings
Ingredients:
4 zucchinis
¼ cup olive oil
½ cup parmesan cheese
¼ cup pine nuts
Salt and pepper

Directions:
1. Shred your zucchini into long thin noodles with your spiralizer.
2. Heat the olive oil in a skillet and add the pine nuts until toasted, about 5 minutes.
3. Add the zucchini noodles. Toss in the oil until warm and coated.
4. Cover with parmesan cheese and combine.
5. Serve warm with salt and pepper to taste.

Cheesy Baked Zucchini Noodle Casserole

Yield: 4 servings

Ingredients:

4 large zucchinis

1 teaspoon kosher salt

2 cups Italian sausage, cut into small pieces

1 tablespoon olive oil

3 garlic cloves, minced

2 medium onions, thinly sliced

1 cup crushed tomatoes

1½ cups assorted cheese (parmesan, pecorino, and mozzarella)

½ teaspoon cayenne pepper

Some fresh basil leaves, chopped

Directions:

1. Peel zucchinis and spiralize them. Sprinkle with salt and let them stand on a strainer for 15 minutes to drain excess water. Set them aside in a large bowl.

2. Heat a saucepan over medium heat and add the sausage pieces. Brown slightly and remove from heat.

3. Heat the olive oil in another pan. Add minced garlic and sliced onion and sauté until slightly browned.

4. Add the crushed tomatoes and sausage pieces and let the mixture simmer for about 5–6 minutes.

5. Season with salt, as needed, then add the zoodles and toss well, using two spoons.

6. Transfer the mixture to a casserole dish. Top with grated cheese and sprinkle on cayenne pepper.

7. Preheat oven to 400 degrees F and bake for 25–30 minutes.

8. Garnish with basil and serve.

Baked Butternut Squash Pasta

Yield: 6 servings

Ingredients:

2 medium-sized butternut squashes

2 tablespoons olive oil

2 tablespoons butter, melted

1 teaspoon nutmeg

1 cup ricotta cheese

1 cup bacon, crumbled

1 cup mozzarella cheese

½ cup parmesan cheese

Directions:

1. Preheat oven to 350 degrees F.

2. Use the spiralizer to create thick squash noodles. Toss them with olive oil, butter, nutmeg, and ricotta cheese.

3. Pour into a baking dish and cover with bacon and remaining cheeses.

4. Bake for 40 minutes, until the cheese is bubbling and the top is brown.

5. Serve hot.

Spicy Cucumber Noodle Pasta

Yield: 4 servings
Ingredients:
4 large cucumbers
1 tomato, chopped
2 handfuls of fresh kale
4 tablespoons olive oil
2 tablespoons red wine vinegar
2 teaspoons crushed red pepper flakes
1 teaspoon garlic powder
Salt and pepper

Directions:
1. Use your spiralizer to turn the cucumbers into long, thick noodles.

2. In a bowl, combine the cucumber noodles with the tomato and kale. Top with the oil, vinegar, red pepper, and garlic powder.

3. Toss to combine and add salt and pepper to taste.

Carrot and Chicken Pasta

Yield: 4 servings
Ingredients:
4 large carrots
1 chicken breast, cooked and cubed
4 tablespoons tahini
4 tablespoons olive oil
2 lemons, juiced
2 cloves garlic, minced
3 tablespoons ginger, grated
2 tablespoons tamari
¼ cup sesame seeds
¼ cup sunflower seeds
1 cup fresh parsley, chopped

Directions:
1. Create noodles out of the carrots using your spiralizer. Sauté them in the olive oil for 5 minutes with the chicken, until warm.

2. While the carrot noodles are cooking, combine the tahini, lemon juice, garlic, ginger, and tamari in a bowl. Whisk until everything is blended. Toss on top of the carrot noodles while they are still in the pan.

3. Sprinkle with seeds and parsley and serve.

Carrot Pasta with Creamy and Zesty Garlic Sauce

Yield: 4 servings

Ingredients:

3 large carrots
1 tablespoon extra-virgin olive oil
1 tablespoon tahini
4 tablespoons lemon juice
1 tablespoon ginger, minced
½ teaspoon sea salt
2 garlic cloves, minced
A handful of parsley
¼ teaspoon ground pepper
1 tablespoon toasted sesame seeds
2 tablespoons toasted peanuts
2 tablespoons toasted walnuts

Directions:

1. Wash, pat dry, and peel carrots. Create noodles out of the carrots using your spiralizer and set aside in a large bowl.

2. In another bowl, whisk together olive oil, tahini, lemon juice, ginger, salt, garlic, parsley, pepper, sesame seeds, and peanuts.

3. Pour this sauce on top of the spiralized carrots and toss well.

4. Garnish with toasted walnuts and serve.

Sweet Potato Pasta Combo

Yield: 4 servings
Ingredients:
6 ounces whole grain linguine noodles
2 sweet potatoes
½ pound ground turkey
4 cups fresh spinach
1 apple
1 cup walnuts, crushed
¼ cup olive oil
Salt and pepper

Directions:
1. Boil the linguine noodles in a pot of salted water until al dente.

2. Use your spiralizer to create long noodles out of the sweet potato and apple.

3. In a skillet, sauté the ground turkey in the olive oil until brown. Add the spinach and keep on heat until wilted.

4. Put the sweet potato and apple noodles in a bowl and cover with the turkey and spinach mixture. Toss to combine.

5. Top with crushed walnuts and salt and pepper.

Pasta with Eggplant and Pear

Yield: 4 servings
Ingredients:
12 ounces whole grain pasta
1 small eggplant
2 pears
¼ cup olive oil
½ cup red wine vinegar
1 garlic clove, minced
1 tablespoon fresh parsley, chopped
1 small shallot
¼ cup thinly shaved pecorino cheese
½ cup walnuts, chopped
2 tablespoons honey
Salt and pepper to taste

Directions:
1. Cook the pasta in a large pot of boiling water. Drain, then set aside.

2. Use the spiralizer to create long, thin shavings of eggplant and pears. Add shavings to the drained pasta and toss until combined.

3. In a separate bowl, combine the olive oil, vinegar, garlic, parsley, and shallot. Add to the pasta and mixture and stir to combine.

4. Top with pecorino cheese and walnuts, drizzle with honey, and season with salt and pepper to your liking.

Paleo Pasta Puttanesca

Yield: 4 servings
Ingredients:
4 large parsnips
1 tablespoon coconut oil
1 large onion, finely chopped
3 garlic cloves, minced
4 large anchovy fillets
1 tablespoon capers
½ cup olives
1 cup tomatoes, diced
½ teaspoon salt
1 tablespoon red chili flakes
1 tablespoon lemon juice
A handful of fresh parsley

Directions:
1. Create noodles out of the parsnips using your spiralizer. Place them in the strainer for a few minutes until the excess water has drained off.

2. Heat the coconut oil in a saucepan. Throw in the onion and garlic, and sauté until slightly tender.

3. Add the spiralized parsnips and cook for 15–20 minutes over medium heat until they are softened.

4. Chop the anchovies, capers, and olives and add them to the saucepan. Mix well.

5. Add the diced tomatoes, salt, chili flakes, and lemon juice and cook for 5–6 minutes.

6. Transfer the pasta to a large plate and garnish with chopped parsley. Serve hot.

Pasta recipes can easily be created with your spiralizer. You can combine pasta with veggies that you turn into noodles, or you can use only the veggies for a low carb dish that looks like your favorite noodles. These pasta recipes will make excellent dishes for lunch, dinner or even a healthy snack that fills your vegetable requirements for the day.

Chapter 3: Salad Recipes for The Spiralizer

Salads are fresh, delicious, and easy to identify as full of vegetables, fiber and all the nutrients and antioxidants that you count on to stay healthy. Your spiralizer will help you create seasonal salads that are high on taste and low on calories. There's no need to stand at the counter chopping veggies for your salad bowl. The spiralizer will keep everything more efficient, which gives you some variety when you're choosing what goes into your salad. These salad recipes will be favorites that you visit time and time again.

Greek Salad with Spiral Cukes

Yield: 3 servings
Ingredients:
2 cucumbers, spiralized
½ cup Kalamata olives, chopped
½ red bell pepper, chopped
½ green bell pepper, chopped
½ red onion, sliced thin
½ cup feta cheese crumbles
2 tomatoes, chopped
½ cup olive oil
¼ cup red wine vinegar
1 lemon, juiced
1 teaspoon fresh oregano
1 teaspoon fresh parsley
1 teaspoon fresh rosemary
Salt and pepper

Directions:
1. Spiralize the cucumbers and combine them in a large bowl with the olives, peppers, onion, tomato, and feta cheese. Toss until all the ingredients are combined.

2. In a small bowl, whisk the olive oil, vinegar, lemon juice with the herbs and salt and pepper.

3. Cover the veggies with the dressing and stir everything together.

Crunchy Asian Salad

Yield: 6 servings

Ingredients:

2 carrots, spiralized

1 head of Napa cabbage, coarsely chopped

½ cup green onions, sliced

1 cup slivered almonds

¼ cup sesame seeds

2 tablespoons soy sauce

¼ cup olive oil plus 1 tablespoon olive oil

¼ cup white vinegar

2 tablespoons sugar

Directions:

1. Use the spiralizer to make long, shredded carrots and toss those with the cabbage and green onions.

2. In a pan over low heat, toast the almonds and sesame seeds in 1 tablespoon of oil. Remove from heat when everything looks toasted and begins to brown.

3. In a small bowl, whisk together the olive oil, vinegar, and soy sauce. Add the sugar and stir.

4. Pour the dressing over the salad and top with the almonds and seeds.

Power Salad with Roasted Chickpeas

Yield: 4 servings
Ingredients:
1 bowl of chickpeas, rinsed
1 tablespoon extra-virgin olive oil
¼ teaspoon sea salt
Pepper to taste
½ teaspoon cumin
1 teaspoon red chili flakes
½ teaspoon dry mango powder
3 large carrots
1 large zucchini
¼ cup fresh basil leaves

Directions:
1. Preheat the oven to 400 degrees F.
2. In a bowl, combine chickpeas with olive oil, salt, pepper, cumin, red chili flakes, and dry mango powder, and toss well.
3. Pour the mixture over a greased baking tray, and bake for about 40 minutes, until the chickpeas are slightly tender.
4. With a spiralizer, cut thin ribbons of carrots and zucchini. Set aside for 10 minutes, then drain the excess water.
5. Add the drained veggies to the chickpea bowl and toss well.
6. Serve chilled.

Sweet Beetato Salad

Yield: 4 servings
Ingredients:
2 sweet potatoes
3 beets
¼ cup green onions
¼ cup pumpkin seeds
¼ cup olive oil
1 teaspoon garlic powder
2 limes, juiced
Sea salt

Directions:
1. Use your spiralizer to turn the sweet potatoes and beets into curly ribbons. Toss with the green onions and the pumpkin seeds.

2. In a small bowl, combine the olive oil, lime juice, and garlic powder.

3. Cover the beets and sweet potatoes with the dressing and combine.

Spicy Thai Chicken Zucchini Noodle Salad

Yield: 4 servings
Ingredients:
1 large zucchini
1 large carrot
1 cup cherry tomatoes
1 teaspoon toasted sesame seeds
1 small scallion, finely chopped
½ avocado, diced
1 cup diced chicken pieces
Some cilantro leaves

Dressing:
1 tablespoon sunflower seed butter
1 teaspoon soy sauce
1 tablespoon lemon juice
¼ teaspoon salt
A pinch of ground pepper

Directions:
1. Wash the zucchini and carrot, and pat them dry with a paper towel.

2. Spiralize the veggies into long, thin, noodle-like strands. Let stand for 15–20 minutes, then drain the excess water. Add the veggies to a large bowl.

3. Add cherry tomatoes, toasted sesame seeds, chopped scallion, and avocado, and toss.

4. Heat a saucepan over medium heat, and add the chicken pieces. Sauté for 2–3 minutes until slightly brown.

5. Add these chicken pieces to the spiralized veggies.

6. In another bowl, whisk together all dressing ingredients.

7. Pour dressing on top of the salad and mix again.

8. Garnish with chopped cilantro, and serve.

Spinach Salad with Apples and Strawberries

Yield: 2 servings

Ingredients:

8 ounces fresh spinach leaves

1 apple

1 cup strawberries

¼ cup chopped red onion

2 ounces goat cheese, crumbled

¼ cup walnuts, chopped

¼ cup almonds, sliced

3 tablespoons olive oil

2 tablespoons red wine vinegar

Salt and pepper

Directions:

1. Use your spiralizer to create thin shreds of apple.

2. Chop the strawberries and combine the fruit with the spinach leaves. Toss with goat cheese, red onion, walnuts, and almonds.

3. Drizzle olive oil and vinegar over the salad, and season with salt and pepper to taste.

Spiralized Sesame Noodle Salad

Yield: 4 servings
Ingredients
1 large seedless cucumber
1 large carrot
1 medium zucchini
4 cups of baby spinach
1 cup of green peas
½ cup almonds, roasted and chopped

Dressing:
¼ cup white wine vinegar
2 tablespoons almond butter
2 tablespoons soy sauce
1 tablespoon honey
1 tablespoon sesame oil
1 teaspoon ginger, minced
1 garlic clove, minced
1 tablespoon toasted sesame seeds
1 teaspoon red pepper flakes
½ teaspoon salt
Pepper to taste

Directions:
1. Wash the cucumber, carrot, and zucchini and pat them dry. Use a spiralizer to cut thin, noodle-like slices and set them aside in a bowl. Mix in spinach.

2. Add green peas and toasted almonds, and mix well.

3. Add all dressing ingredients to a bowl and whisk to combine.

4. Add the dressing mixture to the sliced veggies and toss.

5. Refrigerate for an hour, and serve cold.

Warm Potato Salad

Yield: 2 servings
Ingredients:
2 russet potatoes
2 tablespoons olive oil
Salt and pepper to taste
¼ cup mayonnaise
1 tablespoon Dijon mustard
1 teaspoon soy sauce
1 teaspoon dried oregano
2 eggs, boiled, peeled, and chopped
¼ cup red onion, chopped

Directions:
1. Preheat the oven to 450 degrees F.
2. Put the potatoes through your spiralizer. Toss with olive oil and pour into a roasting pan. Sprinkle with salt and pepper.
3. Bake for 20 minutes, until crispy.
4. In a small bowl, combine the mayonnaise, mustard, soy sauce, and oregano.
5. Pour that mixture over the potatoes, then add the eggs and onion.
6. Mix until well combined.

Fantastic Fruit Salad

Yield: 2 servings
Ingredients:
1 cup blueberries
1 cup strawberries, sliced
1 cup green grapes
1 pear
1 apple
1 lemon, juiced
2 bananas
1 cup cantaloupe

Directions:
1. Use your spiralizer to shred the apple and the pear.
2. Add those fruits to a large bowl with the berries, grapes, bananas, and cantaloupe.
3. Squeeze the lemon juice over the fruits and stir.

Spiralized Beetroot, Corn, and Feta Salad

Yield: 4 servings

Ingredients:

1 tablespoon butter

1 cup sweet corn kernels

4 large beetroots, peeled

2 tablespoons walnuts, toasted

¼ teaspoon salt

¼ teaspoon ground pepper

1 tablespoon lemon juice

¼ teaspoon cumin

2 tablespoons extra virgin olive oil

1 cup feta

A handful fresh parsley leaves

Directions:

1. Heat butter in a saucepan over low heat. Add the sweet corn kernels and sauté for 5–7 minutes, until slightly tender. Set aside in a bowl.

2. Spiralize the beetroots into long strands. Add them to a large bowl. Chop the roasted walnuts and add them to the beetroots. Season with salt and pepper.

3. Add lemon juice, cumin, and extra virgin olive oil, and give it a good mix.

4. Crumble the feta and add it on top of the salad.

5. Garnish with chopped parsley and serve.

Gluten-Free Chicken Salad

Yield: 4 servings
Ingredients:
1 large carrot
1 large seedless cucumber
1 cup bok choy
Salt and pepper to taste
2 medium chicken breasts, cooked and sliced
Some mint leaves
¼ cup peanuts, roasted and roughly chopped

Dressing:
4 large tablespoons lemon juice
2 tablespoons fish sauce
1 tablespoon honey
1 small red hot chili, finely chopped
1 garlic clove, minced
1 tablespoon coconut oil

Directions:
1. Wash the carrot, cucumber, and bok choy thoroughly and pat them dry.
2. Spiralize each of the veggies into long strands and let them stand for 15–20 minutes. Drain excess water and set aside in a large bowl. Season with salt and pepper.
3. In another bowl, combine the lemon juice, fish sauce, honey, chopped chili, minced garlic, and coconut oil and mix well.
4. Mix the dressing with the veggies and toss well.
5. Top with sliced chicken, mint, and peanuts.
6. If you wish, you can refrigerate the salad for an hour before serving.

These salad recipes will work well as meals, side dishes and snacks. Take advantage of your spiralizing technology and bring a new look, texture, and taste to your standard salads. When it comes to salads, your spiralizer will become just as essential as your chopping knives and your salad bowl.

Chapter 4: Breakfast Recipes with Your Spiralizer

Breakfast provides an excellent opportunity to fill up on your fruits and vegetables. The spiralizer can be a resourceful tool when it comes to making tasty, healthful recipes that your whole family will enjoy eating. If your breakfast routine generally includes grabbing a pastry or a cup of coffee on your way out the door, consider upgrading to a meal that includes fresh foods, good fats, and powerful proteins. These breakfast recipes have the potential to change your whole day.

Hash Browns with Sausage

Yield: 3 servings
Ingredients:
½ pound ground turkey sausage
4 red potatoes, peeled
3 tablespoons olive oil

¼ cup fresh parsley
Salt and pepper

Directions:

1. Heat the ground turkey in a skillet until crumbled and cooked through. Remove from the pan and set aside.

2. Use the spiralizer to shred the red potatoes into long curls.

3. Add the olive oil back to the skillet and place the potato curls there, leaving them to cook for about 5 minutes. Toss the potatoes in the skillet until they become crispy.

4. Add the sausage back into the pan and combine.

5. Serve with salt, pepper, and parsley.

Sweet Potato Hash with Egg

Yield: 4 servings
Ingredients:
3 large sweet potatoes
1 tablespoon canola oil
2 tablespoons butter
1 pound chicken sausage, chopped
1 cup button mushrooms, chopped
½ cup water
½ teaspoon salt
1 teaspoon red chili flakes
4 large eggs, fried
½ teaspoon ground pepper

Directions:
1. Wash the sweet potatoes and pat them dry. Spiralize them and add them to a strainer. Let the excess water drain.
2. Heat canola oil in a saucepan. Add the sweet potato noodles to the pan and sauté for 10–12 minutes, until they start to tenderize. Set aside in a large bowl.
3. Melt butter in the same saucepan and add sausage pieces to it. Cook them for 7–8 minutes, until slightly brown.
4. Add chopped mushrooms and continue cooking for 5–6 minutes over medium heat.
5. Add the water, salt, and red chili flakes and stir. Simmer for 5 minutes.
6. Add sweet potato noodles and toss them for 2 minutes.
7. Transfer the mixture to breakfast bowls top with fried eggs.
8. Sprinkle with ground pepper and serve.

Scrambled Eggs with Veggies

Yield: 2 servings

Ingredients:

4 eggs

2 tablespoons milk

¼ cup bell pepper, chopped

¼ cup red onion, chopped

1 zucchini

3 tablespoons olive oil

Salt and pepper

Directions:

1. Use a spiralizer to shred the zucchini into long noodles.

2. Heat the olive oil in a skillet and add the zucchini strips, onion, and bell pepper. Cook for 5–6 minutes.

3. Whisk the eggs with the milk and add to the pan, scrambling with the veggies in the skillet. Combine everything until the eggs are cooked.

4. Season with salt and pepper.

Spiralized Potato and Egg Nest

Yield: 3 servings
Ingredients:
3 large potatoes
1 medium onion, finely chopped
2 tablespoons vegetable oil
½ teaspoon salt
½ teaspoon ground pepper
3 large eggs
3 tablespoons parmesan cheese, grated
1 tablespoon chives, chopped

Directions:
1. Preheat oven to 400 degrees F.
2. Spiralize the potatoes and let them stand for 10 minutes. Drain excess water and set aside in a large bowl.
3. Add onion, vegetable oil, salt, and pepper and mix well.
4. Grease a baking tray with some oil. Transfer the mixture to the tray.
5. Bake for about 25 minutes, until the potatoes turn brown and crisp.
6. Remove from oven, crack eggs on top, and bake for an additional 10 minutes.
7. Garnish with grated cheese and chives and serve.

Zucchini and Tomato Breakfast Pizza

Yield: 3 servings
Ingredients:
3 medium zucchinis
2 eggs
1 cup cherry tomatoes
1 cup sun-dried tomatoes
¼ teaspoon salt
¼ teaspoon pepper
½ cup olives, chopped

Directions:
1. Preheat oven to 350 degrees F.
2. Using the spiralizer, slice the zucchini to get long strands. Sprinkle with salt and put them in a strainer to drain the excess water. Set aside in a bowl.
3. Crack the eggs into the same bowl. Add salt and pepper and combine.
4. Transfer the mixture to a greased baking tray.
5. Top with cherry tomatoes and sun-dried tomatoes. Sprinkle chopped olives and grated cheese on it.
6. Bake the pizza for about 15 minutes and serve.

Fruit Parfait

Yield: 4 servings
Ingredients:
1 pear
1 apple
3 cups vanilla yogurt
½ cup mandarin orange segments
½ cup blueberries
2 tablespoons honey

Directions:
1. Use the spiralizer to shred the apple and pear.
2. Spoon the yogurt into two bowls and top with the apple and pear ribbons, as well as the orange segments and blueberries.
3. Drizzle on honey and serve.

Persimmon and Pomegranate Bowl

Yield: 2 servings

Ingredients:

1 cup pomegranate seeds

2 persimmons

2 ripe bananas, mashed

1 tablespoon chia seeds

1 teaspoon vanilla

¼ cup water

Directions:

1. Allow the chia seeds to soak in the water for 15 minutes.

2. Spiralize the persimmons and place in a bowl. Peel the pomegranates and remove the seeds.

3. Mash the bananas with a fork in a separate bowl and add the chia seeds and water.

4. Layer the persimmons and pomegranate seeds on top of the banana mixture.

Boiled Eggs with Sweet Potatoes

Yield: 2 servings

Ingredients:

3 eggs

1 large sweet potato

¼ cup olive oil

1 teaspoon garlic powder

2 sprigs fresh rosemary

Salt and pepper

Directions:

1. Preheat your oven to 425 degrees F.

2. Spiralize your sweet potato and toss the noodles with olive oil, garlic powder, rosemary and salt and pepper.

3. Spread the noodles out on a rimmed baking sheet and roast for 15 minutes.

4. Boil the 3 eggs and peel after they've cooled. Slice the eggs and serve them on top of the sweet potato noodles.

5. Add more salt and pepper to taste.

Breakfast Lasagna

Yield: 4 servings
Ingredients:
½ pound breakfast sausage
4 eggs
2 carrots
2 potatoes
2 zucchinis
2 tablespoons olive oil
½ red onion, sliced
½ cup mushrooms, sliced
1 cup mozzarella cheese
½ cup parmesan cheese
Salt and pepper to taste

Directions:
1. Preheat oven to 375 degrees F.
2. Cook the breakfast sausage in a saucepan and use a fork to crumble it into small pieces.
3. Scramble the eggs and combine with the sausage crumble in the pan.
4. Use your spiralizer to create shreds of carrots, potatoes, and zucchini. Toss with olive oil, onions, and mushrooms.
5. Coat the bottom of a casserole dish with cooking spray. Cover the bottom with the vegetables, then add the sausage and egg mixture on top. Top with mozzarella and parmesan.
6. Sprinkle with salt and pepper and bake for 30 minutes.

Smoked Salmon Breakfast Scramble

Yield: 4 servings
Ingredients:
2 large sweet potatoes
¼ teaspoon salt
¼ teaspoon ground pepper
2 tablespoons coconut oil, divided
4 pieces smoked salmon, sliced
1 cup collard greens, chopped
¼ teaspoon garlic powder
4 large eggs, slightly beaten

Directions:
1. Preheat oven to 400 degrees F.
2. Spiralize the sweet potatoes and drain the excess water. Sprinkle with salt, pepper, 1 tablespoon coconut oil, and mix well
3. Place the sweet potatoes on a baking tray and bake for 15 minutes. Transfer to a large plate.
4. Heat the remaining coconut oil in a saucepan. Add smoked salmon, collard greens, and garlic powder, and fry for 4–5 minutes.
5. Add the eggs to the mixture and cook for 3–4 minutes.
6. Transfer this mixture on top of the sweet potatoes and serve.

These breakfast recipes include everything you need to get a good start in the morning. Whether you like eggs, sausage, or something vegetarian, your spiralizer can help you create fast, fresh, and delicious meals that won't leave you hungry an hour or two after you eat. Experts have always said breakfast is a crucial component to good health, so make it count.

Chapter 5: Main Course Recipes Using a Spiralizer

Main course recipes are good to keep around, whether you want to make something special or you just need a handful of go-to meal plans for the week. Using your spiralizer, you can turn these main course recipes into fast and easy favorites. To reach your healthy eating goals, most experts recommend that you try to fill most of your plate with vegetables. These dishes help you do just that.

Veggie Spaghetti & Meatballs

Yield: 4 servings
Ingredients:
½ pound ground beef
½ pound ground pork
4 zucchinis
2 cups tomato sauce
1 onion, chopped
2 cloves garlic, chopped
1 teaspoon dried oregano
1 teaspoon dried rosemary
1 teaspoon dried basil
¼ cup milk
1/3 cup Italian breadcrumbs
3 tablespoons olive oil
Salt and pepper

Directions:
1. Preheat the oven to 375 degrees F.
2. Mix the meats with the dried oregano, rosemary, milk, and breadcrumbs. Add milk and salt and pepper. Roll the

meat into small balls and place on an ungreased baking sheet. Bake in the oven for 30 minutes.

3. In a saucepan, heat the olive oil and cook the garlic and onion for about 10 minutes. Add the tomato sauce and allow it to simmer.

4. When the meatballs are done, add them to the sauce and stir. Let the sauce simmer for 20 minutes and add more salt and pepper if necessary.

5. Use the spiralizer to shred the zucchini. Place it in a bowl and toss with the sauce and meatballs.

Quick Bacon Shrimp Zucchini Noodle Scampi

Yield: 3 servings
Ingredients:
3 slices of bacon
1 tablespoon olive oil
2 garlic cloves, minced
12 shrimps, shells removed
1 teaspoon red pepper flakes
½ teaspoon salt
2 shallots, minced
3 medium zucchinis, peeled and spiralized
Ground pepper to taste
4 tablespoons lemon juice
Zest of one lemon
2 tablespoons dried parsley

Directions:
1. Heat a large saucepan and cook the bacon over medium heat until crispy. Remove from heat and transfer to paper towels.

2. In another saucepan, heat the olive oil. Add minced garlic and sauté for 2 minutes until slightly brown.

3. Add the shrimp, sprinkle with red pepper flakes, salt, and shallots and sauté for 3–4 minutes.

4. Add the zucchini noodles and toss with the shrimp mixture. Transfer the bacon pieces to the saucepan and cook for 2 more minutes.

5. Sprinkle with ground pepper, lemon juice, and lemon zest and give it a stir.

6. Garnish with dried parsley and serve.

Fresh Fish with Sweet Potato Pilaf

Yield: 4 servings
Ingredients:
4 cod filets (about 2 pounds)
¼ cup olive oil
2 lemons, juiced
3 sweet potatoes
½ onion, chopped
2 cups vegetable broth
1 teaspoon nutmeg
2 sprigs fresh rosemary
Salt and pepper

Directions:
1. Heat a large skillet and sauté the onion in half the olive oil. Once it's translucent, transfer the onion to a saucepan and add the broth, rosemary, and nutmeg. Stir and allow it to simmer.

2. Use the spiralizer on the sweet potatoes and add the noodles to the broth. Bring it to a boil for 2 minutes and then lower the heat.

3. Preheat the oven to 375 degrees F and drizzle the remaining oil over the fish. Sprinkle with salt and pepper and cover with lemon juice. Bake for 20-25 minutes, until done.

4. Drain the sweet potato pilaf and chop the noodles into smaller pieces. Place the fish on top.

Apple Pork Chops

Yield: 4 servings
Ingredients:
4 granny smith apples
¼ cup olive oil
4 boneless pork chops
3 tablespoons fresh rosemary
½ cup butter
¼ cup brown sugar

Directions:

1. Use a spiralizer to shred the apples, and set the ribbons aside.

2. Heat olive oil in a skillet, and cook the pork chops for 6 minutes on each side. Sprinkle with rosemary.

3. In a small saucepan, melt butter and add brown sugar, whisking until combined.

4. Toss the apple ribbons in the sugar and butter until coated.

5. Serve pork chops on top of the apples.

Honey Orange Beef with Stir-fried Sweet Potatoes

Yield: 4 servings
Ingredients:
2 large sweet potatoes
3 teaspoons coconut oil, divided
1 teaspoon minced ginger
¾ pound steak tenderloin, cut into small pieces
¼ teaspoon salt
A pinch of ground pepper

Sauce:
1 cup orange juice
2 teaspoons ginger, minced
2 tablespoons soy sauce
2 tablespoons honey
6 cups of kale, chopped
¼ teaspoon salt

Directions:
1. Peel and spiralize the sweet potatoes.

2. Heat 1 teaspoon of coconut oil in a saucepan over medium heat. Add the spiralized potatoes to the pan and sauté for 5–6 minutes, until barely tender. Remove from heat and set aside in a bowl.

3. In another saucepan, heat 2 teaspoons of coconut oil. Add minced ginger and sauté for one minute.

4. Add the steak pieces, sprinkle with salt, and cook for 7–8 minutes until cooked through. Set aside in a bowl.

Sauce:
1. In a bowl, combine all the ingredients for the sauce, except kale and salt, and mix well.

2. Add it to the pan and bring to a boil. Keep stirring continuously while the sauce is thickening.

3. Add the kale leaves and salt, and cook for 2–3 minutes. Remove from heat.

4. Place the sweet potato noodles on a large plate. Pour kale over, and add the steak pieces on top.

5. Season with ground pepper and serve.

Burgers and Curly Fries

Yield: 4 servings
Ingredients:
4 turkey or beef burger patties
4 burger buns
Condiments of your choosing
6 russet potatoes
¼ cup olive oil
Salt and pepper

Directions:
1. Preheat oven to 400 degrees F, and prepare your grill or grill pan ready for the burgers.

2. Cook the burgers to your liking, and add whatever condiments you prefer.

3. Spiralize the potatoes and toss them in olive oil. Season generously with salt and pepper.

4. Roast in the oven for 30 minutes, or until golden and crispy.

Buffalo Chicken Meatballs with Cauliflower Sauce

Yield: 5 servings
Ingredients:
8 medium zucchinis
½ teaspoon salt
5 cups vegetable broth
5 cups cauliflower
1 tablespoon olive oil
2 teaspoons garlic, minced
1 onion, finely chopped
Ground pepper to taste
2 tablespoons milk

Meatballs:
1 pound ground chicken
½ cup grated mozzarella cheese
½ teaspoon salt
2 cloves garlic, minced
¼ cup rolled oats
1 egg white
Buffalo chicken sauce
1 teaspoon paprika

Directions:
1. Peel the zucchinis and slice them with a spiralizer.
2. Sprinkle salt on the zucchini noodles and let them stand for about 30 minutes. Drain the excess water and set them aside.

Cauliflower sauce:
1. Pour the vegetable broth into a large saucepan and bring to a boil over medium heat.

2. Lower the heat and add the cauliflower florets. Cover and cook for 7–8 minutes, until tender. Remove from heat.

3. Heat the olive oil in a saucepan and sauté garlic and onion for 2–3 minutes.

4. Add the boiled cauliflower florets and stock to the pan. Add pepper and milk, and simmer for 5–6 minutes. Once cooled down, blend until smooth. Set aside.

Meatballs:

1. Preheat the oven to 400 degrees F.

2. In a bowl, combine all the ingredients for the meatball and mix to form a nice dough.

3. Now roll the dough into small balls and place them on a greased baking tray. Bake the meatballs for 15 minutes, until they are brown.

4. Spread the zucchini noodles on a large plate, cover with cauliflower sauce, and place the meatballs on top.

5. Garnish with ground pepper and serve.

Spicy Stir Fry

Yield: 4 servings
Ingredients:
1 pound chicken tenders
2 carrots
1 head of broccoli
1 head of cabbage, chopped
2 Japanese eggplants
2 cloves garlic, minced
3 tablespoons soy sauce
2 tablespoons sesame oil

Directions:
1. Heat a wok and cook the chicken in the sesame oil.

2. Spiralize the carrots as well as the eggplant and the broccoli stem. Toss the vegetables, including the broccoli florets and the garlic into the wok with the chicken.

3. Add soy sauce and stir until everything is cooked and combined.

Zucchini and Spinach Burrito

Yield: 2 servings

Ingredients:

1 teaspoon olive oil

4–5 chicken breasts, cut into chunks

¼ teaspoon salt, divided

Ground pepper to taste

1 teaspoon garlic powder

1 teaspoon onion powder

1 cup spinach, chopped

2 medium zucchinis, spiralized

8–10 small cubes of feta cheese (about ½ cup)

6 cherry tomatoes

½ teaspoon oregano

Directions:

1. Heat olive oil in a large saucepan over medium heat.

2. Season the chicken with salt and pepper, and place them in the pan. Cook the chicken pieces for 3–5 minutes on each side until they turn golden brown.

3. Add the garlic powder, onion powder, some more salt, and give it a good stir. Cook for a couple of minutes.

4. Add the spinach and zucchini noodles and toss constantly for 3–4 minutes, until the vegetables are tender. Remove from heat.

5. Transfer the mixture into bowls and top with cubed feta and cherry tomatoes on top.

6. Garnish with oregano and serve.

Beet and Beans

Yield: 4 servings
Ingredients:
1 can black beans, drained and rinsed
2 large beets
4 cups spinach
4 scallions, sliced
1 teaspoon sesame seeds
1 teaspoon grated ginger
1 teaspoon sesame oil
2 tablespoons rice vinegar

Directions:
1. Heat the beans in a small saucepan.

2. Use the spiralizer to shred the beets into thin ribbons. Toss the beets with scallions, sesame seeds, ginger, sesame oil, and vinegar.

3. Once everything is combined, add the beans and serve on a bed of spinach.

Bikini Bolognese

Yield: 2 servings
Ingredients:
2 tablespoons olive oil
2 cloves garlic, minced
2 cloves garlic, minced
1 small red onion, chopped
1 medium carrot, finely chopped
1 celery stalk, finely chopped
1 tablespoons red pepper flakes
1½ cups crushed tomatoes
1 tablespoon tomato paste
1 teaspoon oregano
½ pound ground turkey
3 large zucchinis, spiralized
¼ cup chicken broth
½ teaspoon salt
1 tablespoons dried basil
Grated parmesan cheese to taste
Ground pepper to taste

Directions:
1. Heat the olive oil in a large skillet. Add minced garlic and sauté until slightly browned. Add chopped onion and sauté for 2–3 minutes until tender.

2. Add chopped carrots, celery, and red pepper flakes and cook for 3–4 minutes over medium heat.

3. Add crushed tomatoes. tomato paste, and oregano, and cook the mixture for 3–4 minutes, until it thickens.

4. Add ground turkey, zucchini noodles, chicken broth, salt, and basil, and let the mixture simmer for 15–16 minutes, until the sauce reduces.

5. Garnish with parmesan cheese and ground pepper, and serve.

Inside-out Ratatouille with Zucchini Noodles

Yield: 4 servings
Ingredients:
2 small potatoes, diced
1 large eggplant, sliced
1 large onion, finely chopped
3 garlic cloves, minced
1 teaspoon sea salt
2 teaspoons oregano
1/3 cup water
4 ripe tomatoes, finely chopped
2 cups chickpeas, cooked
2 tablespoons balsamic vinegar
2 tablespoons olive oil
4 medium zucchinis, peeled and spiralized
Parsley, chopped

Directions:
1. In a saucepan, combine the potatoes, eggplant, onion, minced garlic, salt, oregano, and water. Cover and cook for around 20 minutes, until all the veggies are tender.

2. Remove from heat and add tomatoes. Cover and let stand for 5 minutes.

3. Add chickpeas, balsamic vinegar, and olive oil to the saucepan and cook the mixture for 20 minutes on low heat.

4. Spread the zucchini noodles on a large plate.

5. Pour the ratatouille on top, garnish with chopped parsley, and serve hot.

Within these main course recipes, you can find an easy favorite, whether you are a vegetarian, trying to watch your weight or forever in search of a good burger. The spiralizer can add variety, flavor, and texture to your meals that you've never experienced   before.   Happy   eating.

Chapter 6: Spiraled Snack and Dessert Recipes

The nifty spiralizer machine isn't just for meals and non-carb pastas. It can also be used to create unique and delicious snacks and desserts. You'll have a healthier way to munch between meals, and it's great to know you don't have to give up desserts while you're trying to eat what's good for you. Try these snack and dessert recipes when you're fighting off a craving or in need of something sweet after you eat.

Veggies and Dip

Yield: 4 servings
Ingredients:
2 zucchinis
2 cucumbers
2 carrots
1 red bell pepper
2 stalks of celery
½ cup ranch dressing

Directions:
1. Use the spiralizer to create long strands of zucchini, cucumbers, and carrots.
2. Chop the pepper and celery into strips.
3. Arrange the veggies around the ranch dressing, which you can use for dipping.

Yummy Spiralized Vegetable Wraps

Yield: 4 servings

Ingredients:

1 avocado, peeled and thinly sliced
2 cups spinach, roughly chopped
1 large cucumber, peeled and spiralized
1 large carrot, peeled and spiralized
1 large beetroot, peeled and spiralized
½ teaspoon salt
A pinch of ground pepper
1 tablespoon lemon juice
4 large whole grain tortillas
½ cup hummus
Roasted cashews, halved
Some toothpicks

Directions:

1. In a bowl, combine the chopped avocado with spinach, cucumber, carrot, beetroot, salt, pepper, and lemon juice and toss well. Make sure all ingredients are mixed very well.

2. Lay the tortillas on a large plate. Spread a large spoonful of hummus on each of the tortillas. Sprinkle on some roasted cashews.

3. Fill the tortillas with the veggie mixture. Carefully wrap them into a roll and secure with toothpicks.

4. Serve them along with some additional hummus.

Vegan Collard Green Handrolls

Yield: 4 servings
Ingredients:
2 large carrots
1 teaspoon butter
½ cup sweet corn kernels
1 cup bean sprouts
1 medium onion, finely chopped
1 teaspoon ginger, minced
½ teaspoon sea salt
3 tablespoons lemon juice
1 teaspoon white wine vinegar
1 teaspoon sugar
1 teaspoon red chili flakes
A pinch of ground pepper
4 large collard green leaves
Some toothpicks

Directions:
1. Wash the carrots and pat them dry. Peel and spiralize the carrots. Set aside for a few minutes and drain the excess water. Set aside in a large bowl.

2. Heat the butter in a saucepan and cook the corn kernels for about 4–5 minutes, until tender.

3. Add the corn kernels to the carrots, followed by the bean sprouts, onion, ginger, and salt and mix well.

4. Add the lemon juice, vinegar, sugar, chili flakes, and ground pepper, and toss again.

5. Add the mixture to the saucepan, and sauté for 3–4 minutes.

5. Place the collard greens on a plate. Add the carrot filling in each of the leaves, wrap them, and secure with a toothpick.

6. If you like them cold, you can refrigerate these rolls for a couple of hours and serve them with some fresh cherries.

Paprika Potato Chips

Yield: 4 servings
Ingredients:
2 russet potatoes
¼ cup olive oil
2 tablespoons sea salt
1 tablespoon black pepper
1 tablespoon white pepper
2 tablespoons paprika

Directions:
1. Preheat the oven to 425 degrees F.

2. Use the ribbon blade on your spiralizer to turn the potatoes into thin slices. Toss the potatoes with the olive oil, salt, pepper, and paprika.

3. Spread the chips out onto a baking sheet in a single layer. Roast in the oven for 30 minutes, until they become crispy and golden.

Baked Balsamic Carrots

Yield: 4 servings

Ingredients:

4 carrots

3 tablespoons olive oil

¼ cup balsamic vinegar

Sea salt

Directions:

1. Preheat the oven to 350 degrees F.

2. Spiralize the carrots into thin strips. Load them into a baking dish and cover with the oil, vinegar, and salt.

3. Bake for 10 minutes and enjoy.

Baked Pears

Yield: 4 servings

Ingredients:

2 pears

2 tablespoons butter, melted

1 teaspoon white sugar

2 teaspoons brown sugar

2 cups nonfat vanilla frozen yogurt

Directions:

1. Preheat oven to 325 degrees F.

2. Spiralizer pears into ribbons. Toss in the melted butter until coated.

3. Pour the pear strips into a baking dish and sprinkle with white and brown sugars. Toss to combine.

4. Bake for 30 minutes. Serve over bowls of frozen yogurt.

Spiralized Apple Crumble

Yield: 8 servings
Ingredients:
8 medium apples
1 teaspoon ground cinnamon
1/3 cup brown sugar
Zest of one orange
½ cup orange juice
4 scoops of vanilla ice cream

Crumble:
1 cup almond flour
1 cup rolled oats
1/3 cup brown sugar
A pinch of cinnamon
¼ teaspoon salt
¼ teaspoon nutmeg
4 tablespoons coconut oil

Directions:
1. Preheat oven to 400 degrees F.
2. Wash the apples thoroughly and spiralize them. Set aside in a bowl.
3. Add the cinnamon, brown sugar, orange zest, and orange juice to the bowl and mix well.
4. Grease a baking tray and add the apple mixture.
5. In another bowl, combine almond flour with the rolled oats, brown sugar, cinnamon, salt, nutmeg, and coconut oil and mix with your hands. The mixture should be crumbly.
6. Add this crumble on top of the apples.
7. Bake for 35–40 minutes and serve with vanilla ice cream.

Chocolate Drizzled Apples

Yield: 4 servings

Ingredients:

4 apples

½ lemon, juiced

4 strawberries, sliced

¼ cup cacao

3 tablespoons coconut oil

4 tablespoons maple syrup

¼ cup sliced almonds

Directions:

1. Spiralize the apples and place them in a bowl. Squeeze lemon juice over them to keep them from turning brown while you make the chocolate sauce.

2. In a small saucepan, melt the coconut oil and add the cacao. Stir for 5 minutes until melted and combined. Remove from heat and add the maple syrup. Stir until combined and let cool for 30 minutes. It should thicken.

3. Pour the sauce over the apple ribbons and top with the strawberry slices and almonds.

Spiralized Carrot Pudding

Yield: 4 servings

Ingredients:

3 large carrots

1 tablespoon clarified butter

¼ cup heavy cream

2 tablespoons raisins

¼ teaspoon ground cardamom

4 tablespoons honey

2 tablespoons brown sugar

2 tablespoons almonds, roasted

2 tablespoons pistachios, roasted and shelled

Directions:

1. Wash and peel carrots. Spiralize the carrots into long, thin strands.

2. Melt the butter in a saucepan over medium heat.

3. Add the spiralized carrots and cover. Cook for 7–8 minutes over medium high heat.

4. Pour the cream into the saucepan. Add the raisins and mix. Cook for another 2–3 minutes until the mixture thickens.

5. Add cardamom, honey, and brown sugar and give it a stir. Cover and remove from heat. Let stand for 7–8 minutes.

6. Pour the pudding into bowls and refrigerate for a few hours.

7. Chop up the roasted almonds and pistachios. Sprinkle them on top of the pudding and serve.

Non-Traditional Apple Pie

Yield: 6 servings

Ingredients:

¾ cup flour, divided into 1/4 cup portions

6 apples, peeled

5 tablespoons sugar, separated

1 tablespoon melted butter

2 tablespoons cold butter, chopped

1 teaspoon vanilla

½ teaspoon salt

½ teaspoon cinnamon

½ teaspoon nutmeg

1 teaspoon baking powder

¼ cup water

½ cup buttermilk

Directions:

1. Preheat your oven to 375 degrees F.

2. Use your spiralizer to create thin slices of apple.

3. In a bowl, whisk together the apples, 1/4 cup of the flour, 2 tablespoons of the sugar, melted butter, cinnamon, nutmeg, vanilla, and salt. Spoon into your pie dish and add the water.

4. In a separate bowl, combine the remaining flour and sugar. Incorporate the baking powder and then the chilled butter pieces, using a processor or two spoons. The texture should be coarse. Add the buttermilk and stir until moist.

5. Spoon that mixture over the apple mixture in the pie dish. Smooth everything out so it evenly covers the pie dish, and bake for 1 hour.

As you can see, these snack and dessert recipes are satisfying, delicious and nothing to feel guilty about. Your spiralizer will give you options that keep your snacking interesting. It's also sets a food climate that's better for your body. The time you'll take to prepare these healthful snacks will allow you to anticipate the eating of them. That will help you enjoy your food more mindfully. Whether you're looking for something to snack on while you're watching television or you want a sweet and savory dessert to wrap up a delicious meal, these recipes will deliver on taste.

Conclusion

Learning how to use a spiralizer will improve your plans for cooking and eating, and your overall health will be much better off because of it. All of the excellent vitamins, minerals and nutrients from fresh vegetables and fruits will fill you up with the energy and antioxidants you need to get through the day and keep yourself healthy. Add some of your own favorite flavors to the recipes, because the more you're able to personalize your meals, the more successful you'll be at eating healthy, spiralized food.

Finally, I want to thank you for reading my book. If you enjoyed the book, please take the time to share your thoughts and post a review on the book retailer's website. It would be greatly appreciated!

Best wishes,

Savannah Gibbs

Check Out My Other Books

Mediterranean Diet Cookbook: Easy and Delicious Mediterranean Diet Recipes to Lose Weight and Lower Your Risk of Heart Disease

Clean Eating Cookbook: Quick and Easy Clean Eating Recipes to Lose Weight and Live Healthy